Where We Live

Bangladesh

Donna Bailey and Anna Sproule

STECK-VAUGHN
LIBRARY
A Division of Steck-Vaughn Company

Hello! My name is Malek.

I live in Dacca, Bangladesh.

I help my father run his stand in the market.

We sell lentils, peas, beans, and rice.

2

Dacca is the capital of Bangladesh.
It is a very big city on
the banks of the Burhi Ganga River.
Our house is near the river.

During the monsoon season, from June to
September, it rains hard every day.
The river rises and floods parts of Dacca.
The water often comes into our house, too.

My mother stays at home and
cooks for the family.
We eat a lot of fish in Bangladesh.
My favorite meal is rice, fish, and
a flat bread we call chappatti.

For my coming-of-age celebration when
I was eleven, my mother made spicy
rice pulao and a special dessert.
We also had a rickshaw procession
through the streets of Dacca.

I wore my best clothes and rode with my grandfather.

The rickshaw was covered with flowers
and decorations for good luck.

Afterward, the priest came to our house.

He said prayers and gave me his blessing.

Hindu and Muslim boys both have
coming-of-age celebrations.
Hindus pray together in temples.
Many Muslims pray here at the Star Mosque.
It is the biggest mosque in Dacca.

My brother Hossain is a rickshaw-puller.
He carries passengers around the city
in his rickshaw.

9

Hossain made his rickshaw by himself.
He used pieces of old bicycles,
metal, and wood.
We all tried to help!

A Hindu artist painted pictures
all over the back of Hossain's rickshaw.
The pictures tell stories about the
Hindu gods and about life in Dacca.

Pulling a rickshaw is hard work.
Hossain pedals his rickshaw 30 to 40 miles
around Dacca every day.

Dacca is a busy city, and there are
many rickshaw-pullers in the streets.
The hoods over the seats of the rickshaws
shade the passengers from the sun and
help keep the rain off during the monsoons.

People in Dacca also travel from
place to place by bus, but
the buses are always crowded.
If the bus is full, people sometimes
stand on the outside step.

If you want to cross the river,
a ferry pilot will pole you across
in a flat-bottomed boat.
You need to stand still so you don't fall in!

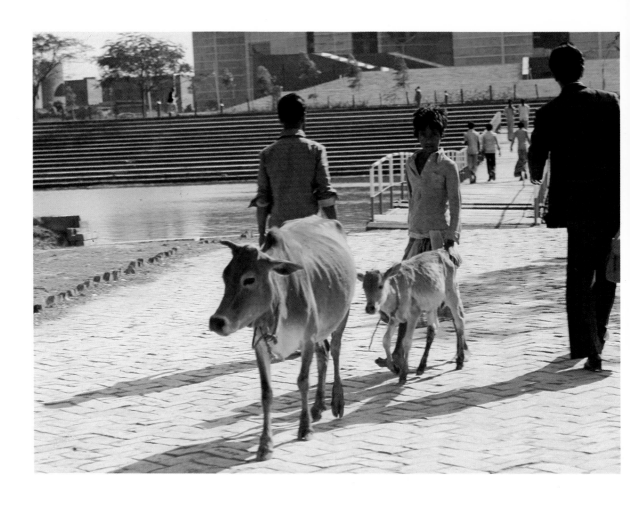

In addition to rickshaws, cars, and buses,
there are many cows in the streets of Dacca.
Cows are sacred to the Hindus so
they are taken care of and allowed
to roam free.

16

My uncle lives in the country.

He sends the crops he grows to Dad
in Dacca.

Dad sells them from his stand in the market.

One year I visited my uncle.

I went up the river on a boat like this one.

There are many rivers in Bangladesh.
In a boat, you can travel almost anywhere
in the country.
Some of the boats are big ferries.

Many boats have flat bottoms to
keep them from getting stuck in the mud
of shallow rivers.
The farmers send their crops to Dacca
in these boats.

Jute is an important crop in Bangladesh.
It is raised for its strong fibers.
These farmers are loading jute
onto a boat.
The boat will take their crop to Dacca.

When there is no wind, the crew
uses long poles to push the boat
through the water.

When there is enough wind, the crew
puts up the sails of the boat.
Then they can sail down the river to Dacca
with the cargo of jute.

The men unload the jute at the factory
in Dacca.
People there use the jute to make rope,
sacks, and wrapping paper.

Many villages along the river
are built on tall poles called stilts.
When the river rises during the monsoons,
the houses on stilts do not get flooded.

This village on the riverbank often
gets flooded during the monsoons.

The village people travel
by boat during the floods.

Some people even live on their boats
all year round.

Sometimes, when the river rises very high,
people must leave their flooded homes
and stay with relatives on higher ground.

Then the flood waters cover the fields.
The mud and silt carried by
the flood waters make the crops grow well.
The farmers can grow three crops a year.

When the floods go down, the farmers
plant their crops.

This farmer has two water buffalo to
help plow his fields.
After plowing, he will plant rice seedlings.
The farmers grow a lot of rice because
everybody in Bangladesh eats rice.

All the men help with the rice harvest.
They tie the rice in bundles and carry it
back to the village.
In the village they will separate
the grains of rice from the straw.

Index

Reading Consultant: Diana Bentley
Editorial Consultant: Donna Bailey
Executive Editor: Elizabeth Strauss
Project Editor: Becky Ward

Picture research by Jennifer Garratt
Designed by Richard Garratt Design

Photographs
Cover: Sarah Ainsile
Colorific Photo Library: 3,4,31 (Penny Tweedie), 9 (Stephen Emery)
Commonwealth Institute Library Services-Compix: title page, 6,7,8,10,11,12,16,23,30
The Hutchison Library: 2,15 (Sarah Errington), 5,14 (Joan Klatchko), 18,21,22,24,25,27,28,29
Robert Harding Picture Library: 13,19,20 (Graham Birch)
Screen Ventures Picture Library: 17 (Sarah Ainsile)
Tropix Photo Library: 26 (R. Cansdale), 32 (N. Lloyd)

Library of Congress Cataloging-in-Publication Data: Bailey, Donna. Bangladesh / Donna Bailey and Anna Sproule. p. cm.—(Where we live) SUMMARY: A child living in Dacca describes everyday life, foods, transportation, occupations, celebrations, and floods in Bangladesh. ISBN 0-8114-2559-2 1. Dhaka (Bangladesh)—Social life and customs—Juvenile literature. [1. Bangladesh—Social life and customs.] I. Sproule, Anna. II. Title. III. Series: Bailey, Donna. Where we live. DS396.9.D3B35 1990 954.92′2—dc20 90-9652 CIP AC

2 3 4 5 6 7 8 9 0 PO 96 95 94 93 9